Time Management

The Simple Modern Guides & Secrets: Successful Individuals Comprehend Time Management And The Art Of Balancing Work And Celebrations

(Exploring And Assessing Your Time Management: An Insight-filled Manual To Revolutionize Your Life)

Adrien Dunlop

TABLE OF CONTENT

Last Thoughts 1

Some Advice On Planning Your Day 13

Useful Illustrations Of The Time Slot Approach 31

Quality Vs. Quantity: Going Beyond "Busy" 51

Is It Just Urgent, Or Is It Really Important? 75

Embracing New Paradigms And Solidifying Change 91

Concentration And Focus 112

The Success Blueprint: Time Management Foundations For A Busy Life 133

Last Thoughts

Thank you for reading this time management book through to the end!

We've looked at various methods, approaches, and resources to support you in making the most of your time, working more efficiently, and striking a good work-life balance.

We'll wrap up this chapter with final thoughts to help you retain what you've learned and offer extra advice.

The Value of Repetition and Practice

Time management skills are a continuous process that requires perseverance and practice.

Developing effective and productive routines takes time, just like learning any other skill.

Be open to trying out various tactics, making necessary adjustments to your plans, and remaining dedicated to improving time management.

Modifying Techniques to Fit Your Lifestyle

Remember that not every tactic discussed in this book will be effective for you.

Everybody has different wants, tastes, and lifestyles.

Please modify the methods and resources presented here to better fit your needs.

Evaluation and Ongoing Enhancement

The ability to manage one's time well is a constant.

As you put the ideas covered in this book into practice, remember to regularly examine and enhance your time management strategy.

When required, try different strategies, and be open-minded to what you may learn from your experiences.

Developing a Well-Being Lifestyle

Recall that effective time management involves more than just increasing productivity.

It also involves striking a good balance between relationships, jobs, personal life, and self-care.

Remember to schedule time for relaxation, pleasure, and self-rejuvenating activities.

Set your priorities in order of importance, and ensure your objectives and goals reflect your values and aspirations.

Your Path

Thanks to this book, You have a strong basis for enhancing your time management skills,

Remember that every person is different; thus, your path to efficient time management will also be unique.

Be open to researching, trying out, and customising tactics to fit your requirements.

The ability to manage your time well can change both your personal and professional life.

You may increase your productivity, efficiency, and fulfilment in all facets of your life with commitment, practice, and dedication.

I appreciate you joining me on this educational and personal development journey.

I hope you keep progressing towards a balanced life and efficient time management.

Juggling Personal and Professional Life

Maintaining excellent mental and physical health and fostering healthy relationships depend on striking a balance between work and personal life. Here are some pointers for managing your personal and professional lives:

1. Make self-care a priority: Keeping a work-life balance requires making self-care a priority. This entails making time for activities like exercise, meditation, or hobbies that enhance physical and mental well-being. Making self-care a priority can help people feel less stressed, have more energy, and generally be healthier.

2. Establish boundaries: Achieving work-life balance requires boundaries between personal and professional lives. This could entail establishing and adhering to specified work hours or days off, defining boundaries with

coworkersor superiors, and refraining from checking work emails or taking work calls during personal time.

3. Develop better time management abilities: People with better time management abilities are more productive with their time, lowering stress and making more time for leisure activities. This can involve assigning responsibilities, establishing timetables or to-do lists, prioritising work, and refraining from multitasking.

4. Learn to say no: Achieving work-life balance requires learning to say no to extra job responsibilities and social engagements, even though doing so might be difficult. Saying no helps people avoid taking on more than they can

handle and free up more time for their interests.

5. Establish realistic goals: Make sure your goals align with your personal and professional lives. To reach such objectives, avoid taking on more than you can manage and develop good time management skills.

6. Take regular pauses: Throughout the workday, taking regular breaks can help you refuel and maintain focus. Make the most of your downtime by doing fun things like going for a stroll or reading.

7. Control your technology usage: Avoid using it too much, especially alone. Establish limits on your use of social media, and don't answer business calls or check emails during your time.

8. Establish a support network: Establishing a support network can assist people in overcoming obstacles related to work-life balance. This can include friends, family, or coworkers who can offer emotional support, assistance with chores for the job or personal life, or counsel and direction.

9. Assess the culture at work: Assessing whether the current position or company is a suitable match may be important if work culture makes it difficult to achieve work-life balance. This could entail looking for a job that offers a better work-life balance or pushing for adjustments to the workplace culture as it exists now.

Although juggling work and personal obligations can be difficult, doing so is essential to preserving happiness and general well-being. You may successfully manage your time and strike a good work-life balance by implementing these methods.

Recognising the Difficulties of Work-Life Balance

For many people, striking a healthy work-life balance can be difficult. The following are some typical obstacles to work-life balance:

1. Overworking: Overworking is one of the biggest obstacles to a work-life balance. Many people experience pressure to put in more hours at work or

bring work home with them, which results in a lack of personal time and elevated stress levels.

2. Lack of time management abilities: This is another issue that makes it difficult to strike a work-life balance. Ineffective time management can result in wasted time, raising stress levels and making it harder to finish tasks.

3. Unrealistic expectations: Some people have high standards for themselves, whether they are in their personal or professional lives. Burnout, tension, and disappointment may result from this.

4. Family and personal obligations: Juggling work and obligations such as caring for ageing parents or children can be difficult. These tasks might take a

long time, making it difficult to find time for personal hobbies.

5. Job requirements: Certain positions require a lot of travel, overtime, or long hours. Finding time for personal interests can be challenging due to these expectations, which can cause stress and burnout.

6. Work culture: It can be difficult to attain work-life balance in some organisations due to the work culture. Finding personal time might be challenging, for instance, in a society that emphasises working long hours or being available all the time.

To properly handle work-life balance issues, it's critical to recognise them.

Achieve a healthy work-life balance by tackling these issues.

Some Advice On Planning Your Day

Developing a plan also takes some trial and error because everyone has different preferences—some of which they may not even be aware of yet. Some people work out in the morning to give themselves the energy boost they need for the afternoon, while others prefer to work out during lunch. Only by giving these minor adjustments a try can you assess how they impact your day. You will ultimately discover the most effective routine for you in this manner.

I've compiled a list of suggestions that help create a schedule.

Arrange the Previous Day/Night

You can plan your days in general with the use of a timetable. It will make a huge difference if you set aside some time at the conclusion of your workday to organise your next day's activities. It will help the following day go more smoothly and enable you to prioritise the activities that require your full focus right now. By doing this, you'll be able to include them in your day without changing the general time of your plans. You won't have to waste time getting organised if you establish the practice of planning the night before. When you arrive at work, you'll know exactly what has to be done. This greatly increases your level of productivity and focus.

Set priorities.

Depending on your preferred working method, you may wish to finish all of the week's major assignments before moving on to minor projects. But you'll also be able to plan shorter assignments that you can complete quickly for a day when you need extra time alone with your family. Avoid scheduling lengthy chores for when you are most likely to become sidetracked or interrupted. The majority of people are more productive in the morning. As a result, you should try to arrange your work so that you may finish the most critical chores first and remain active all day. You will become increasingly aware of how your energy and attention span change daily as you work from home more frequently. You may better organise your schedule and prioritise your tasks by doing this.

This also holds for non-work-related items you want to prioritise in your schedule. Taking your children to school, having breakfast with your significant other, or spending time reading daily are some examples. Using a schedule, you can identify your priorities and ensure you know how to fit your job around them.

Include Exercise in Your Routine

It can be easy to forget that you must be physically active when working from home. Cause you to lose sight of time or your enthusiasm to exercise. It is therefore best to include it in your timetable. After that, it becomes a crucial aspect of your day and enhances your general well-being. Many people who work from home tend to overlook scheduling this. If you don't schedule it, you'll discover that you'll quickly put it off in favour of something else. Exercise is a crucial supplement that can help you feel better overall, have more energy during the day, and reduce stress. It is, therefore, best to include it in your daily routine and not allow work to interfere with it. Consider it a top priority that you fit in around your job.

Remember to Take Breaks

If you worked in an office, you wouldn't neglect your breaks. As a result, when working from home, remember to plan your breaks. People I've known have stated that they would rather work from home without taking breaks. On the other hand, spending a lot of time at a desk is unhealthy. The purpose of breaks is to remind you to move, to let your body breathe in some fresh air, and to provide a mental break. If you skip them, you will feel more exhausted at the end of the day. Your eyes will be tired, your mind depleted, and you won't have as much energy for your loved ones or pets. Taking short pauses during the day will also help you to take care of your pets, spend time with your family, and finish some household duties. As a result, you should remember to factor in breaks because they are equally as crucial as work in your timetable.

Get Rid of Those Boring Tasks

Making a schedule helps you discover and prioritise the tiresome chores that must be completed. Then, you may arrange for them to be completed at a time that frees up your schedule for other things. For instance, you can set a time each morning to make all your weekly phone calls or designate a certain time to respond to your emails. You may develop a routine with these chores and avoid putting them off by using a schedule.

Utilise Management Resources to Assist

You may manage your time with various management tools, as covered in the second chapter. The ability to sync your devices and send reminders can truly help your schedule. This kind of scheduling may be more manageable, particularly if you make a lot of adjustments. If you rearrange things correctly, you won't have to worry about running out of room to write. I also find that adding details to particular tasks on my schedule is helpful. Thanks to this, I don't have to waste time searching for documents because I can easily access everything in one location.

Provide your youngster with positive male role models to help them flourish.

Having no father figure in your child's life does not mean your child lacks positive male role models. It is imperative to acknowledge that the existence of powerful male role models can have a significant effect on your child's growth and offer them insightful viewpoints and direction.

To support this important part of your child's upbringing, consider choosing a male relative or a reliable friend with whom you already have a close bond. This person, who could be your father, brother, uncle, or close friend, can be a dependable mentor and source of support for your child.

Encouraging these connections may take some extra work, but the benefits are enormous. You are giving your child an opportunity to encounter positive male influences directly by allowing them to connect and form relationships with these male role models. Even when a father figure is absent, this exposure contributes to developing a comprehensive view of males.

Your work in fostering these bonds helps your child develop a positive view of men's role in their lives. It guarantees they have a sense of safety, direction, and encouragement as they grow up, providing the groundwork for their social and emotional growth. Ultimately, the enrichment derived from these relationships is priceless in supporting your child's overall development and well-being.

Use your inner power to improve as a mother.

When a father figure is absent from their child's life, single mothers usually struggle to fill the hole that is left. You have very little control over the father of your child, so accepting this reality might be frustrating.

It's important to recognise that, despite your sincere wishes, you cannot force your child's father to parent in a way that conforms to your ideal. Focusing on your parenting skills rather than trying to alter someone else with your limited resources would be considerably more beneficial.

Give yourself time to consider the special traits and advantages you offer your child. Accept that your role as a mother carries much weight and power.

You empower yourself to succeed as a single mother by supporting your child's development, offering emotional support, and creating a loving atmosphere.

Turn your viewpoint to focus on what you can provide for your child. Instead of focusing on the inadequacies of the other parent, concentrate on giving your child the support, affection, and direction they require to flourish.

By doing this, you give yourself the ability to be the greatest mother you can be, and your child will surely gain from your constant commitment and uplifting impact.

In case you get locked out, keep an extra key hidden outside.

A basic but essential safety precaution for single mothers is to conceal an extra key outside in a safe place only accessible to you and your kids. Anyone can become locked out of their home anytime; life can be unpredictable.

Having a spare key close at hand helps ease tension and alleviate worries about safety in such circumstances, particularly if your kids are with you.

But it's crucial to pick a hiding place wisely, making sure it's not visible or simple for outsiders to get to.

By taking this precaution, you can control who has access to your house in an emergency and feel secure knowing you have a backup plan to quickly re-enter your house and protect your family.

Join forces with other single mothers.

Collaborating with other single mothers on projects like carpooling or organising potlucks can be helpful for various reasons. Above all, it establishes a helpful network where lone mothers may rely on one another for practical and emotional assistance.

For instance, potlucks provide time- and money-saving meal options, which lessen the daily cooking workload. Furthermore, splitting up chores like carpooling helps save time and energy and ease the logistical difficulties of juggling kids' schedules.

Working together with other single mothers creates a supportive network, lessens feelings of loneliness, and offers support when needed.

It's a win-win situation that encourages productivity, delegating, and closer relationships among group members, making the experience of single parenting easier to handle and less daunting.

Be patient and optimistic in raising a single child.

Being a single mother, especially in the early years of your child's life. Setting reasonable expectations for your child and adjusting duties and obligations based on age and developmental stage is critical.

This method establishes the foundation for cultivating tolerance and keeping a cheerful environment in your house.

Being a single parent has its own set of challenges, including the lack of a support system for when you reach your breaking point.

Consequently, it's critical to recognise your triggers and create useful coping mechanisms to maintain composure. Shouting is rarely productive and frequently causes distress for you and your child.

Instead, consider using strategies to keep your composure, such as inhaling deeply and counting to 10 carefully before acting.

When you reach ten, you'll frequently discover that your feelings have subsided, and you two may even start laughing about the whole thing.

Additionally, use these difficult times to have frank conversations with your child. Tell it like it is, and be open about how you feel and why you might be having trouble with a certain situation.

The sympathetic response from your youngster may surprise you.

In addition to creating a peaceful home atmosphere, exercising patience and keeping an optimistic mindset also provides a good example for your child.

It strengthens your caring and supporting relationship with your child while teaching them resilience and important life skills.

Ultimately, you can handle the highs and lows of being a single mother with grace and courage if you maintain your composure and outlook.

Useful Illustrations Of The Time Slot Approach

The time slot method, which assigns discrete time blocks, or "slots," to various jobs and activities throughout the day, has become a crucial approach to time management. In actual use, this approach can be varied and used in many situations. We'll utilise several examples to demonstrate its application, showcasing its adaptability and utility.

Project Management for Labour

Consider yourself a graphic designer who is juggling multiple tasks at once. You can set aside specific times during the workday for each assignment to help you manage your time efficiently. For instance, you may set aside the first two hours of the day to design a logo for a client, and the following block of time, focus on creating a brochure for a different client. By dividing up your time this way, you may concentrate on one activity at a time rather than multitasking and its detrimental effects on productivity.

scholarly research

Assume you are a college student who has to juggle multiple classes. By adopting the time slot strategy, you may set certain blocks of time to study each subject. For instance, you may focus on a difficult subject that calls for your whole attention in the mornings and less demanding work or exam preparation in the afternoons. You might also designate weekly times to complete assignments like writing essays or conducting research.

Everyday and Individual Tasks

The time slot approach can be used for everyday and private activities besides work and school. For instance, you may schedule some time in the morning to work out before spending some time on breakfast and getting ready for the day. Before bed, you may set aside some time to read or learn something new. You're more likely to persist with these hobbies if you set up particular periods for them and they become a part of your routine.

Managing Emails and Meetings

Workflow interruptions from emails and meetings are prevalent in the workplace. On the other hand, the time slot strategy allows you to choose a certain time of day to complete certain chores. To focus on your important activities for the remainder of the day, you could, for instance, limit the times you check and answer emails to first thing in the morning and last thing at night.

A Moment of Relaxation

It is important to remember that the time-slot strategy is not limited to productive pursuits. These time slots are crucial for preserving equilibrium and averting burnout. These can be as simple as going for a stroll, drinking coffee, reading a book, or practising meditation. These illustrations demonstrate how the time slot method can efficiently plan your day so that you can manage a variety of obligations without feeling overburdened. This approach is a flexible time management tool that may be tailored to your own needs and circumstances. You can generally raise your level of contentment with life, attain a better work-life balance, and increase your productivity by employing it effectively.

Chapter 6: Choosing and Applying Techniques

Things to Take Into Account While Choosing a Strategy

Choosing a time management technique that works requires careful consideration and planning. Every person has a different connection with time. Therefore, it's important to understand that no technique works the same way for everyone. Numerous aspects must be considered to select the best course of action. This thorough analysis will increase the likelihood of successfully implementing the selected approach.

The nature of the activity or task at hand should be taken into account first. Different strategies may be needed for tasks requiring a high level of focus compared to those that are more automatic or usual. For instance, the Time Slot technique might be more appropriate for repetitive chores requiring less concentration than the Pomodoro approach, which is perfect for focused, intense jobs.

Your current habits and personal work rate make up the second component. While some people work best in longer, uninterrupted workdays, others prefer shorter workdays interspersed with regular breaks. You might choose a plan that fits your innate patterns by knowing your work rate.

Third, the setting and context of the piece are as crucial. You might want techniques to lessen distractions if your workplace is noisy or has frequent interruptions. Conversely, you might be able to choose from a wider range of tactics if your workplace is calm.

It's also critical to evaluate workload and deadline compliance. While certain tactics could be more effective at ensuring deadlines are fulfilled, others might be more suited for managing a large workload. Your needs can be best served by choosing the technique that best fits your workload and time constraints.

Next, the necessary degree of flexibility needs to be taken into account. While some techniques are more flexible and can adapt to changes and unforeseen circumstances, others are more inflexible and demand strict adherence to a predetermined plan. If you have to be highly flexible in your professional or personal life, choosing a plan that will let you adjust as things change could be a good idea.

The degree of control you have over your time is the sixth thing to consider. While some people are free to arrange their time as they see fit, others are severely limited by rigid job schedules or family obligations. You can successfully apply a wider range of techniques the more control you have over your time.

The approach you select may also be impacted by using time management software. For instance, if you are accustomed to utilising a digital agenda, you might favour integration-friendly tactics with that particular tool. However, if you would rather have a simple, handwritten to-do list, you can choose methods that don't involve sophisticated technology.

Lastly, it's critical to consider your personality and learning preferences. Certain time management techniques might align with how some people learn and think. Knowing how you organise and process information might provide important hints about what methods could be most effective for you.

The nature of the task, your work rate, your workload and deadlines, the amount of flexibility needed, your control over time, the use of time management tools, and your personality and learning style are all important considerations when choosing an efficient time management strategy. By considering each of these factors, you will be better equipped to select a plan to boost your output and contentment with time management.

A bad answer could be the result of discipline concerns. This failure will harm both the person and other people.

A disciplined person knows how to develop an optimistic outlook. This helps the person make decisions and analyse scenarios.

Intelligence hurts, even if he doesn't desire someone uncontrollable.

He puts everyone around him in danger in addition to doing such harm to himself.

As a result, a deliberate mental attitude is needed. Consequently, the person reacts suitably to the environment in which they live. Disciplining the mind to cultivate this kind of mental attitude is essential.

One of the most important skills we need to have to succeed in society is the correct attitude. It leaves a lasting impression on other people as well.

Enhanced Better concentration through focus

To be a productive member of society, one must exercise mental and physical self-control. According to scientific studies, regular practice leads to the development of a lovely, healthy physique. Exercise also improves your ability to think positively, according to research.

Practising discipline may synchronise your thoughts and goals with your physical form. It is easier to control our thoughts and emotions so we can concentrate on our objectives.

For the most part, a student's punishments are more severe. You plan your workload to balance your physical and mental needs; since they are both in good physical and mental health, this significantly enhances their academic achievement. It will be easier for anyone with good discipline, especially students, to achieve their goals in life. Thus, a relationship exists between the student and the discipline. The ability of the mind and body to focus on what needs to be done is enhanced by discipline.

Regardless of rank, anyone who works in a shop or a corporate environment may benefit from discipline.

Being in charge of your everyday activities enhances your capacity to focus on your work. This increases your output in anything you do.

enhanced mental well-being

improved mental well-being

Worry and hopelessness are major problems for people in today's society. They have to do something, even if it would be unreasonable to hold them solely responsible for their circumstances. You may increase the significance of discipline in your life by engaging in self-discipline practices.

Research indicates that panic attacks are more common among teenagers who struggle with self-control. There are undesirable outcomes of panic attacks. They are a cause of worry and hopelessness because of these memories.

Because emotions are the only things that can break this closed loop, responses to situations can differ.

Controlling these kinds of emotional outbursts could make someone more patient and thoughtful. Discipline liberates your intellect but makes it stagnant. Sometimes, a person who has a disorganised life will not accomplish anything.

In addition, an old saying states that a wilderness is the devil's workplace. Problems may arise if your ideas are not managed and kept free.

You run the risk of developing problems and depression if you're idle. As mental health improves, discipline becomes more important.

These ideas might make it more difficult to pursue peace. These difficulties could be intellectual, psychological, social, or a combination. These people find it difficult to interact with others because they are so worried about their circumstances.

When you imagine the worst, you tend to overthink situations. Those who are disciplined may help others get out of difficult situations and benefit themselves. Therefore, these difficulties and barriers may extend beyond disciplinary mindsets. People such as these are beneficial to society's mental health.

enhances interpersonal harmony and improves focus

For a society to function properly, discipline is required. Many terrible things would occur if there was no law and order. These kinds of actions will undermine society's capacity to function.

To prevent such incidents in society, social life needs to be controlled. Establishing rules and conventions makes a community easier to live in.

Individuals pick up the skill of harmonious social coexistence. These rules prevent interpersonal conflicts or injustices.

As previously stated, an individual in control knows how to respond in different circumstances. He understands the consequences of his actions. Someone who has resided in a corporation understands the importance of discipline.

In the hamlet, Jack gained a reputation as a leader and problem-solver after that day. He had reached his potential and regarded himself as responsible for the village's well-being. He demonstrated that you could accomplish great things and benefit the world around you if you held yourself accountable and accepted responsibility for your actions.

The hamlet prospered as Jack got older and taught the following generation the lessons he had learnt. Forever thankful to Jack for his guidance and teaching them the value of taking responsibility for one's actions, the villagers flourished and led happy, long lives.

Jack's tale serves as a reminder that one of the most important components of personal development is taking responsibility for oneself. It entails accepting accountability for the results of your choices, actions, and behaviour and those acts themselves. You may accomplish your goals, better yourself, and reach your full potential by holding yourself accountable. You can also gain the respect and credibility of others.

Quality Vs. Quantity: Going Beyond "Busy"

It's time to reconsider production in a society that exalts busyness. Being busy is not the same as making progress or feeling fulfilled. In this chapter, we'll examine ways to prioritise high-impact tasks for best outcomes and engage in meaningful activities as we explore the idea of quality versus quantity.

Reevaluating the Myth of Busyness
The "busy" culture frequently misleads us, making us feel better about ourselves than we are and ignoring the real significance of our actions. Being busy can result in aimlessness, inefficiency,

and fatigue. It's critical to distinguish between meaningful chores that advance our progress and ones that merely keep us in a loop.

Think of two people: Alice and Bob. Throughout the day, Alice jumps around, answers emails, attends meetings and crosses things off her to-do list. On the other hand, Bob concentrates on a small number of important initiatives that support his objectives and gives his all to genuinely important ones. Bob produces better-quality results, while Alice seems busy because he is thoughtful about where he spends his time and energy.

Techniques for Taking Part in Important Activities

The foundation of meaningful activity is engagement. Committing to whatever you're doing, whether business, hobbies, or personal endeavours, improves your experience and outcomes.

To become more involved:

Being mindful: Remain mindful to be in the present. You're likelier to create excellent work and feel satisfied with your efforts when committed.

Alignment of Passion: Find pursuits that are consistent with your ideals and areas of enthusiasm. Your work will always be of higher quality when you are passionate about what you do.

State of Flow: Aim for the flow state where you're so engrossed in the work that time flies by. This intense focus produces remarkable outcomes.

Optimising High-Impact Tasks to Achieve Maximum Outcomes

Not every assignment is made equally. According to the Pareto Principle, sometimes called the 80/20 rule, 20% of efforts provide 80% of the results.

To use this idea:

Setting priorities: Sort the assignments by importance to see which ones will affect your objectives most. This keeps you from becoming weighed down by little tasks that have little bearing on your goals.

Eisenhower Matrix: Sort jobs according to their significance and urgency. Pay attention to the high-impact, non-urgent jobs that are in the "important but not urgent" quadrant; they are the ones that propel advancement.

Deep Work: Adopt the mindset of setting aside uninterrupted, concentrated time to work on challenging projects. When you work deeply, you can achieve better results than when you work superficially or distractedly.

Reaching Greatness via Superiority

Let's say you own a garden. Cultivating a few carefully selected and well-tended plants will yield a beautiful landscape, but packing it full of plants won't. Similarly, you should tend to your productivity garden by picking high impact jobs with deliberate thought.

You'll find renewed fulfilment in your achievements when you change your focus from quantity to quality. Recall that improving performance is more important than increasing output. Aim for excellence in your endeavours as you work through the tactics in this chapter. Your path to significant accomplishments is marked by intentionality, purpose, and a dedication to achieving genuinely significant results.

Chapter 5: Collaboration and Effective Communication

Developing effective communication is more than just enhancing our social interactions. It allows us to communicate our needs and the value we provide to a project more effectively. Furthermore, you can expand your skill set by applying some of the concepts described in this chapter. In light of that, I encourage you to use this chapter in novel ways. Start with your group and see if anything resonates with your personal life! Similarly, keep in mind that life and work are not distinct entities. Because of this, the abilities you employ in your personal life can frequently be applied to productive communication in the business.

Simplifying Channels of Communication

Attending a two-hour meeting that would have been as informative as an email is a common example of poor management. Thankfully, there is a way to reduce this. We can lead more effectively and use our time wisely if we discern. But before we can become aware of this, we need to comprehend the variety of available instruments, particularly in the post-pandemic environment, where communication has undergone a significant transformation. Before the crisis, remote work was an uncommon choice, but it soon gained popularity. For me, it was difficult because my office was five minutes away. But a few of my coworkers expressed gratitude for not having to spend hours of their day travelling, saying it made them feel prepared for work. In addition, our redesigned communication methods were my biggest support during the pandemic. With fewer and fewer pointless calls, I could communicate more easily and complete my responsibilities without worrying about a fuzzy application not being fully functional.

But regardless of whether your team is located in the same building or works remotely, you must use the right communication tools. Zoom and Microsoft Teams, for instance, provide the ability to make video calls. However, anyone with experience working with both platforms would tell you they are very different animals. Teams can use many channels. It seems less like an occasional call and more comprehensive.

Although Zoom appears simple, it is a really useful tool when needed. With most of the features you would anticipate, you can arrange a call, send out invitations, and run the full meeting in less than two minutes. I've worked in most workplaces that combine these technologies, so you must assess which ones are appropriate for each situation and make that decision.

You may generally be a minimalist. Slack, for instance, is ideal for brief messages because it is simple to use and lightweight. However, some teams require frequent document exchanges. In situations like this, I favour teams. Look over the app's documentation if you're ever unsure. Frequently, we are unaware of their whole feature set. The usefulness of keyboard shortcuts is another. You should spend some time learning these, in my opinion. They'll reimburse you sooner than you anticipate. Combining one app with emails, a few face-to-face meetings, and the appropriate project management tools should be simple. After that, conceal any program you are not using. Maintaining a neat desktop is simple.

You've chosen a communication platform, then. That's good. This is the tough part now. Recall how I discussed boundaries and the difficulty of setting them up early in the book. Recognising that you can't reply to every text immediately is another boundary.

Ensure team members know your expected arrival time and when you'll probably be out to lunch.

It would be advisable for you to motivate your group to follow suit. It's quite basic, but it works. Expect more organised team communications shortly, both inbound and outbound. This is just one of several practical tips you may take to make sure you're managing clearly. Based on studies, consider the following guidelines to abide by:

After making your ideas clear, send them.

To achieve your desired communication goal, modify how you speak and present it.

Make your message situation-appropriate.

When it's wise, speak with people one-on-one about bigger gatherings.

Being a leader is more than just speaking. Develop your listening skills.

Give your employees something of worth. This means considering their opinions and areas of interest.

Make sure you get comments. We appreciate your team's thoughts and queries.

Lastly, exhibit congruence.

An alternate issue you might experience is a constant barrage of emails. The first step is to set aside an afternoon to make up. Get rid of anything unnecessary and save anything you might find later. The greatest place to start is if you can have your inbox almost completely reset. You can now use email etiquette. Periodically check your email during the day. as a planned event instead of a sudden stoppage. Delete any messages you don't need to see initially when you check. These might be anything from calendar invites to spam to simple mishaps. It should be clear from their titles what they are. If responding would benefit the other participants in the chain and take no more than three minutes, please do so. You can file everything else. Most email providers let you build smart folders that apply specific filters, which makes it much easier to view pertinent messages if you're tech-inclined.

Knowing when to respond is another useful tip. Many of the issues have already been rectified by the time they reach me. Or I would only be able to say yes or no in answer. These two situations don't warrant an email. Inform your direct reports and those to whom you have assigned tasks if you discover they are updating you too frequently. Re-establish the communication-related milestones. Also, let them know you trust them and their qualifications.

Let's discuss what makes a meeting valuable. An insignificant update regarding a project's progress, for instance, isn't it? Consider the benefits of meetings rather than viewing them as the standard solution. Put otherwise, under what circumstances would calling a meeting be more effective than not calling one? You can use a straightforward technique to remove most pointless meetings by delaying calling them until they pass four filters. First of all, don't rely just on instinct. Evaluate the circumstances and determine the best course of action. If you're still considering holding a meeting, consider if you can do the task at hand without assistance from others or if you need their advice. In the latter scenario, a meeting is not necessary! Ask whether real-time input is required when you realise you need it. This usually serves as the largest filter for me. If not, just send an email and wait for a response from your colleagues. Finally, decide if a call or a chat would be more appropriate for your needs. Analyse after you've responded to each question in sequence. Plan if a meeting is required! It is in everyone's best interest to keep the meeting as brief and clear as possible while you do this.

Chapter 6: Choosing Whether or Not to Be

Small business owners spend much time considering and choosing their options. All Three Faces of Time can be disrupted by agonising over choices.

Unable to sleep at night might violate tertiary time, leaving you exhausted and less productive.

Not many small business owners have examined how they make decisions. How do you come to your decisions?

• Compile all available data about your topic.

• Verify that you have accurately identified the problem or obstacle posed by your choice. Look for the root of the problem rather than just its symptoms.

• Take into account how timely your choice is.

• Think about what happens if you don't decide.

• Get other opinions on your choice.

- Create a strategy and carry out your choice. Techniques for Making Decisions

Technique of Consequences

Technique of Fantasising

When we make decisions, we frequently confine ourselves to where we are. Although this is useful, you can be open to new ideas by practising a basic fantasising approach.

Try imagining yourself in your place to help you be more open-minded. If you had an infinite budget, how would you, for instance, approach things differently?

What is the best possible result that your choice will yield?

Mentoring Approach

Having mentors you can bounce ideas off when you are stuck on a decision can make all the difference. Locate trustworthy individuals who are not involved in your company's day-to-day operations. These folks are good decision-makers; they don't have to work in your sector. Create relationships and stay in touch; keeping a list of these folks nearby can save you time when you need them most.

The In Their Shoes Method

Consider the viewpoints of all those impacted by the decision or engaged in its making. Ask those concerned, if necessary, how they think various decisions will affect them.

Deductive Reasoning

Consider the larger picture and the various results of your choices. Based on your prior experience with comparable circumstances and other people's experiences, draw judgements as much information as you can should go into your hypothesis.

Cost-Benefit Evaluation

Calculate the potential advantages and weigh the costs of different options. This should be one of the first techniques after all other relevant ones have been exhausted.

Advantages and Dangers

Charles Kepner and Benjamin Tregoe devised one systematic approach to decision-making. Using a matrix procedure, this method forces users to consider all advantages and hazards. There is much more to benefits and hazards than just gain or loss. Among these are client retention, morale among staff members, hiring and firing decisions, cost implications, and avoiding legal trouble, to mention a few.

The Skill of Ceasing

Stop and consider when this decision needs to be made to prevent drawing incorrect conclusions or gathering information. Think about the effects of delaying your decision. This will allow you more time to gather information and double-check facts.

Value of Decision-Making

To decide, calculate the cost. Often, the costs of research performed to make judgements have been more costly than the consequence of the given option made. Weigh the time and manpower that will be needed to make the decision. Know the value of making a decision.

Group Consensus: Bring everyone involved together and have a discussion. You could even get a democratic vote from the group to consider the majority opinion. Pros and Cons

It is one of the oldest but still most reliable decision-making strategies. Draw two columns and list the benefits of a decision on one side and the disadvantages on the other. Weigh the results.

Is It Just Urgent, Or Is It Really Important?

What comes next? You deal with this problem multiple times a day, from when you wake up until you go back to sleep. How you respond to such questions will determine how you live your life. All those answers add up to your existence. As we saw from the exercise in the previous chapter, you can and should decide the importance of such matters to keep some control over your life. Many things won't fit on your planner, but you can schedule and prepare for the ones you can anticipate. Many of the questions only accept yes/no responses.

Is it better to roll over immediately or wait a little longer?

Do I have to eat breakfast? In what way should I eat? Should I have a shower? What kind of clothing should I wear?
Are you saying that these aren't choices? Of course, at least during the workday, you wake up at roughly the same time every day. Of course, you either eat breakfast or not.
Do you have an option?
Think about the matter of clothes. What you wear says a lot about your social status and how you view others.
I announce that I'm prosperous and respectable if I show up to work in a suit

and shirt. If I wear a tattered sweatshirt and cutoffs, I might still be a good citizen, but I'm heading to the garden or the car wash. Lipstick, black leather, and spike heels all send very different messages.

You retort that, although this is accurate, your options are limited. The topic of what to wear to a business meeting is one of social conventions. Indeed.

You still have an alternative, though. You consciously choose to do that at some point. You are still exercising your free will even if you now choose your level of dress (instead of the exact tie or earrings) out of habit or default.

Learning to assume some responsibility for your decisions and increasing your awareness of them are the keys to efficient time management.

We're not saying you should wear cutoffs or leather to work.

We're not suggesting that you make choices about your oral hygiene, such as which quadrant of your mouth to brush first, what toothpaste to use, or how to hold the toothbrush when using that hand. You should perform these tasks rote as long as your routine serves you well. (And oh, the mayhem when, for example, carpal tunnel syndrome in your dominant hand forces you to learn how to brush your teeth "wrong-handed.)

But you are not doing yourself any favours if you make every decision out of habit.

The phone's buzzing dilemma

Imagine that you are using a phone while working in an office. (That wasn't too far to stretch). (Again, in my opinion, not a truly original visioning achievement.) Pretend the phone rings. Are you going to answer it? Yes, you do have options, particularly if you have voice mail or can let the call go to another phone, but most of us just answer ringing phones without giving it any thought. (Recall Pavlov's eager canines? And not even a biscuit is given to us as we ring our rings!

Without knowing who is on the other end of the phone, the most vital piece of information you may have to determine is whether to pick up the buzzing device, but let's make it simple by providing you with the caller ID. Assume the person you are speaking with is your living partner or significant other. We'll refer to them as the "SO" from now on. The individual who means the most to you personally on earth. Would you like to answer the phone at this moment?

Yes, of course, but let's face it: you're working at your job, very busy, in the middle of something important, under pressure, and, to be honest, you kind of wish you could have known what would be discussed before you decided to begin, don't you? Not even a phone ID can help you there.

But before you decide whether to answer the phone or let it ring through, I will tell you exactly what your SO wants to talk about utilizing the power of the made-up scenario. It works either way; however, SO is a guy in this case.

● Case A: SO is calling to inform you that he feels the left side of his face is completely devoid of feeling and that he might faint at any time.

● Example: You've just talked long with his sister Carol, who lives in Oregon. She is having a terrible time with her oldest child, Bobby, who was recently expelled from school after it was discovered that he had marijuana in his locker. Carol and your other, who are unsure how to help, are upset. He wants to talk to you about it.

● Case C: He wants to talk about your union. You two fought last night and were still furious when you left for work this morning. A couple of things need to be resolved right now.

● Case D. Nothing unique. He just wants to communicate.

So, will you be picking up that phone call? The choice is yours.

If you choose to stay away from him, I promise there won't be any repercussions, and your significant other won't find out.

Case A is unquestionably true, right? You'll not only take the call but drop what you're doing and run home to take him to the hospital. It's a simple decision but also a terrifying and potentially terrible situation.

In this case, Case D may also be a straightforward choice. We'll talk more later.

Case B presents greater difficulties. You are interested in the soap opera currently playing in Oregon and Carol and Bobby. You are even more concerned since your significant other is sad and preoccupied with a family matter. However, there is nothing that you can do at this time (or perhaps ever). Furthermore, you really should get ready for that crucial appointment that is in fifteen minutes.

Does my voicemail seem to be ringing?

One could argue that Case C is considerably more difficult. Your relationship with your SO is the most important thing in your life. But this is not the place, time, or format for a meaningful discussion. It's probably not help to rehash the fight from last night, and it might even get worse. You must admit that you are a little miffed that he called now, given how busy you are. Nevertheless, avoiding this is generally preferable, so you may discuss the issue later.

Chapter 11: Law of Parkinson's

Have you ever observed that some people accomplish amazing amounts of work in a short time while others take an eternity to finish even the most basic tasks? Parkinson's Law explains this phenomenon: "Work expands to fill the time available for its completion." Put another way, even if a task doesn't take a lot of time, you will spend more time on it the more time you have to finish it.

British historian and novelist Cyril Northcote Parkinson initially proposed Parkinson's Law in a 1955 essay in The Economist. Parkinson's essay outlines a fictitious government bureaucracy that expands in size despite lacking tasks. He contends that this is because bureaucracies, like all organizations, are governed by Parkinson's Law, which states that an organization's workforce will always find ways to increase output, even redundant.

Parkinson's Law also pertains to an individual's productivity, although it is frequently connected to bureaucracy and organizational inefficiencies. The longer you give yourself to finish a task, the more probable you will become sidetracked, put off doing it, and waste time on unimportant things. This may result in a drop in output and feelings of overwhelm and dissatisfaction.

Making the most of your time is crucial to counteract Parkinson's Law's harmful impacts. The following advice can help you do that:

Give strict deadlines.

Setting strict deadlines for yourself is essential to combating Parkinson's Law. You'll be forced to concentrate and pay closer attention if you give yourself less time to finish a task and are less inclined to spend it on unimportant things. You'll be able to accomplish more in less time by doing this and become more productive.

For instance, he is known for giving his workers strict timelines. He thinks that by encouraging people to step outside of their comfort zones, this strategy helps them become more creative and productive.

Divide the work into manageable portions.

Segmenting highly complex activities into smaller, more doable ones is another strategy to counteract Parkinson's Law. This can lessen your sense of being overwhelmed and simplify assigning each assignment to a precise, realistic deadline.

Olympic swimmer Michael Phelps, for instance, is well known for breaking down his training into manageable, incremental goals. Every day, he would concentrate on a single element of his technique, like his breathing or stroke, and progressively attempt to improve at it.

Make use of time-blocking

A time-management strategy called "time-blocking" entails allocating particular time blocks for various jobs or pursuits.

For instance, author and efficiency specialist Cal Newport suggests managing your weekday with time-blocking. He advises setting out certain time slots for emails, conferences, and concentrated work and viewing each slot as a "meeting with yourself."

Get rid of distractions.

By consuming important time and attention, distractions can worsen the consequences of Parkinson's Law and be a significant barrier to productivity.

For instance, internet investor and entrepreneur Naval Ravi Kant suggests disconnecting all your computer and phone notifications and even putting your phone in a different room when you're working. By doing this, you can prevent yourself from becoming distracted by email, social media, or other sources of distraction.

Recall that time is money and that each minute lost is one that we cannot get back. Parkinson's Law can be overcome, allowing us to regain control over our time and allocate it to priorities, whether as a business owner or a learner.

Embracing New Paradigms And Solidifying Change

It's essential to embrace and accept change to overcome resistance and negativity. When everyone knows about the upcoming changes, there won't be any cause for dread. Given that humans are naturally flexible, it is your responsibility as a leader to encourage, uplift, and support your team members.

Since outdated ideas and contemporary settings frequently collide, adjusting and implementing cutting-edge strategies for contemporary workplaces is critical.

Results-Only Management. The results-only management model is one such strategy that emphasises worker productivity over presence. Because employees may select when, where, and how they work, this approach promotes trust and brings out the best in them, allowing them to concentrate on meeting goals rather than wasting time on menial activities.

For instance, a software company that adopted a results-only management approach greatly boosted productivity and employee happiness.

Workers valued freedom and flexibility, which improved output and eventually raised the company's earnings.

The Revolution in Wellbeing. The wellness revolution, which emphasises the value of employees' physical and emotional wellbeing, is another contemporary workplace trend. Employers may empower their workers to have a better work-life balance by adopting decisions prioritising the health of the entire workforce.

Prioritising staff wellness can significantly impact a business, leading to enhanced job satisfaction and productivity. For instance, a marketing company saw performance after implementing flexible scheduling, mental wellness days, and fitness programmes.

Because these new models have different priorities and expectations from traditional methods, contemporary methods emphasise outcomes, flexibility, and well-being more than traditional methods, which emphasise presence and strict timetables.

In conclusion, to overcome resistance and adjust to the changing nature of the workplace, it is imperative that one embrace and accept change. Organisations and workers can benefit from a healthy work environment that firms cultivate by concentrating on employee wellness and using results-only management. It's time to move past outdated ideas and seize the opportunities the contemporary workplace presents.

Accepting Change and Succeeding in the Face of Uncertainty

Handling the Change Winds

Accepting change is the only way to move forward because it is unavoidable. However, how can one overcome resistance and embrace novel approaches to thinking and doing? The following tactics can assist you and your group in adjusting and prospering:

Sustain a Positive Attitude

It all starts with how you think about change. A positive outlook will motivate your team and assist you in overcoming obstacles. They are more inclined to trust and adhere to your advice if they perceive you as a self-assured leader receptive to fresh perspectives.

For example, the CEO of a well-known retail company had infectious joy and excitement as the company switched to e-commerce. The company's effective transformation was facilitated by the employees' motivation to acquire new skills and adjust to the demands of the digital marketplace.

Make Change Work for You: Examine how alterations may present fresh chances for development and advancement. If you have this mentality, you will see obstacles as chances to grow and achieve. For instance, a manufacturing company used automation and optimised its production process in response to heightened competition. They were able to concentrate on innovation and market expansion in addition to becoming more efficient due to this shift.

Review and Make New Objectives

A change could have an impact on your long-term goals and aspirations. Give your objectives a second look and adjust them to reflect the current situation. This approach has the potential to be empowering, rekindling your enthusiasm and drive to reach even bigger goals.

For instance, a software development business discovered fresh prospects in the developing domain of artificial intelligence. They increased the scope of their product offerings and obtained a competitive advantage by establishing new objectives in line with this technology.

How better time management might enhance mental wellbeing

Time management and mental health have a mutually reinforcing and intricate link. It has the potential to enhance mental wellbeing. Here are a few ways that effective time management might enhance our emotional wellbeing.

Decrease in tension and worry.

Ineffective time management frequently results in anxious and stressful circumstances. Our stress reaction takes over as work piles up, deadlines approach, and time appears to be slipping away. This can have detrimental long-term implications on our mental health. We may lessen these stressful circumstances and decrease our anxiety through efficient time management. Making a plan for the day, the week, or the month and sticking to it gives us a clear idea of what has to be done and when which helps us feel less overwhelmed.

Enhanced self-worth

Additionally, efficient time management can increase our confidence and sense of self. We feel competent and accomplished when we do our assigned responsibilities and reach our goals. This can increase our self-assurance that we can manage obligations and difficulties, which can benefit our mental health.

More time for personal hygiene

Effective time management may guarantee that we always have time for self-care, which is crucial for maintaining our mental health. We can ensure that there is always time in our schedule for leisure and recreational activities by organising and prioritising our tasks. During this self-care period, we can rejuvenate our energies, unwind, and enhance our emotional health.

enhanced quality of sleep

Our ability to sleep can be affected by the tension and worry that come from time management issues. We can raise our sleep quality by managing our time well to lower these stress levels. Our physical and mental wellbeing depend on getting enough sleep, and getting too little sleep can.

encouraging harmony between one's personal and work lives

Proficient time management can furthermore aid in fostering a sound equilibrium between one's personal and professional lives. We may ensure that both aspects of our lives get the required attention by setting out specified work and personal activities hours. Maintaining a healthy equilibrium between our personal and work lives is crucial for maintaining mental wellbeing and averting burnout.

constructing resilience

Last but not least, time management can aid in developing resilience, which is critical to mental health. The capacity to adjust to and overcome hardship is resilience. Effective time management enables us to adjust to challenging circumstances, modify our plans of action when things don't go as planned, and bounce back from setbacks faster.

To sum up, effective time management can significantly enhance our mental health in several ways. We may enhance our quality of life and mental health by lowering stress, raising self-esteem, scheduling self-care time, fostering a good work-life balance, and developing resilience in life. But it's crucial to remember that every person is unique, so what suits one could not suit another. Finding the time management techniques that work best for us is crucial since time management is a process that requires ongoing learning and adaptation.

3.2 Apply ThePomodoro Method

Francesco Cirillo created the well-known Pomodoro Technique for time management in the late 1980s. The goal of this technique is to increase productivity, decrease distractions, and help you stay focused by dividing your work into small bursts known as "pomodoros" (Italian for "tomatoes") interspersed with short rests. The method comes from the tomato-shaped kitchen timer Cirillo used as a student.

Using the Pomodoro Technique is as follows:

1. Select an assignment: Choose a project or job you wish to work on. This could be anything from writing, learning, or doing a work task.

2. Set a twenty-five-minute timer: You can change the duration of the Pomodoro interval to suit your needs and preferences. However, the standard interval is 25 minutes. Use this time to work solely and completely focused on the selected task.

3. Complete the assignment: Don't multitask or be distracted as you start. During the Pomodoro, if you think of anything else you need to complete, simply write it down and return to work.

4. Take a little break: Take a break after the five minutes have elapsed. Stretch, drink, or engage in any other fun and soothing activity at this period. Taking a break helps you mentally recharge and avoid burnout.

5. Carry out the procedure again: Work for another 25 minutes in Pomodoros, with 5-minute breaks. Take a longer break—15 to 30 minutes—after finishing four Pomodoros to allow for a longer rest and renewal.

6. Monitor your development: Record the amount of Pomodoros you finish and the tasks you work on at each interval. This might assist you in assessing your

productivity and modifying your time management plan as necessary.

Increase productivity and divide work into digestible parts. You can maintain motivation and engagement while steadily advancing towards your objectives by working in brief, concentrated bursts and taking regular pauses.

3.3 Blocking and Organising Time

Two similar time management strategies are time blocking and time boxing, which entail scheduling chores and activities into designated time windows. With these techniques, you may improve focus, divide work into digestible portions, and manage your time more effectively. An outline of each method is provided here:

Blocking out time:

Setting aside time in your calendar or planner for particular tasks or activities is time blocking. You can establish a disciplined daily routine that will assist you in maintaining attention and organisation by giving each task a designated time window. Here's how to put time blocking into practice:

1. Determine what needs to be done: List everything you have to do in the next day or week.

2. Calculate the time needed: Determine the approximate time needed to finish each task.

3. Set up time blocks: Give each task a distinct time slot on your schedule. Ensure you allot enough time for each work, considering any deadlines or priorities.

4. Follow your timetable: Don't multitask or allow outside distractions within any certain time block. Instead, give your full attention to the subject at hand.

5. Modify as necessary: Make the necessary adjustments to your schedule if you discover that you have overestimated or underestimated the amount of time needed for a task.

Time-Boxing:

Like time blocking, time boxing entails assigning a specific amount of time to each activity, regardless of when it is finished. This method can assist in avoiding perfectionism and procrastination while motivating you to work more productively. Here's how to put time boxing into practice:

1. Determine what needs to be done: List everything you have to do in the next day or week.

2. Establish a deadline: Assign a specific amount of time to every task. This should instil a sense of urgency while providing a reasonable estimate of the time needed to do the work.

3. Plan time slots: Put specified times on your schedule for each task and ensure you finish them within the allotted time frames.

4. Work within the time limit: Give attention to the task at hand during each time box, and try to do it in the allocated time. If the task is incomplete, either go on to the next one or set aside more time.

5. Evaluate and make adjustments: Review your performance after the day or week and make necessary changes to your scheduling or time estimations.

You may increase productivity and concentration and split things into manageable portions using time boxing and time blocking. You can establish an organised routine that promotes productive and concentrated work by designating particular time intervals for chores and activities.

Concentration And Focus

B. Establishing a happy workplace

Encouraging work environments is critical for productivity and employee happiness. The following advice can help you establish a productive workplace:

Promote open communication: Promote direct communication between management and staff. In the workplace, this can foster a sense of belonging and trust.

Express gratitude: Thank your staff for all of their efforts and contributions. Raising spirits can be achieved with as little as a simple "thank you" or acknowledgement for a job well done.

Encourage employees to prioritise their emotional and physical well-being and take breaks to foster a work-life balance. Stress levels can drop, and productivity can rise as a result.

Encourage staff members to cooperate and exchange ideas to foster collaboration. This can foster a culture of positivity and teamwork at work.

Promote professional development: Motivate staff members to learn and acquire new abilities. They may remain motivated and involved as a result of this.

Consider yourself the manager of a small company, for instance. You may promote open communication and a healthy work atmosphere by encouraging staff members to express their thoughts and conducting frequent team meetings. Employees can receive a thank-you email or recognition for their accomplishments during meetings when you show appreciation for their hard work. Encourage collaboration by sponsoring team-building exercises and flexible work schedules to promote work-life balance. Facilitate professional growth by granting access to workshops and training courses.

Improving employee satisfaction and productivity requires fostering a positive work environment. You may establish a collaborative and happy work environment by promoting open communication, expressing gratitude, encouraging work-life balance, encouraging teamwork, and supporting professional development.

C. Controlling stress and upholding a healthy way of life

In addition to being beneficial for general wellbeing, stress management and upholding a healthy lifestyle can increase productivity at work. The following advice can help you manage stress and have a healthy lifestyle:

Use relaxing methods: Utilise methods of relaxation to focus better and manage stress.

Regular exercise: Frequent exercise can enhance physical and mental health and help lower stress.

Consume a balanced diet: Stress can be decreased, and energy levels raised by lean protein.

Make time for sleep: Besides being beneficial for general health, getting adequate sleep can increase concentration and productivity at work.

Schedule time for your favourite pastimes and pursuits: You may lower stress and enhance your general wellbeing by scheduling time for your interests and hobbies.

Consider yourself an office worker who is experiencing extreme stress, for instance. During your lunch break, you can practise relaxation and maintain a healthy lifestyle. After work, visit the gym or go for a stroll as a regular form of exercise. Ensure your nutrition is well-rounded by bringing a nutritious lunch and snack to work. Make getting enough sleep a priority by setting aside time each day to go to bed and wake up simultaneously, and schedule in time for enjoyable hobbies like reading or playing an instrument.

In conclusion, leading a healthy lifestyle and controlling stress are critical for general well-being and can boost output at work. Stress levels and boost productivity by applying relaxation techniques, consistent exercise, a well-balanced diet, adequate sleep, and scheduling time for enjoyable hobbies.

Goal Visualisation: Increase drive with precision

Visualisation is a potent tool that increases motivation by enabling the user to see the intended result in their mind. This spiritual warm-up gives you newfound energy to pursue your objectives.

Imagine yourself succeeding.

If you want to succeed, lose yourself in intricate mental scenarios. Engage your senses to make the image as vivid as possible, eliciting the emotions associated with accomplishment.

Overcoming challenges

Provide a graphic representation of the difficulties you may face and potential roadblocks. This fosters resilience and assists you in psychologically preparing for any setbacks.

Establish Segments and Goals: Defy procrastination's hold.

Establishing specific objectives and dividing them into doable steps reduces confusion and offers a path for consistent advancement.

SMART objectives

Establish well-defined goals using the SMART framework (specific, measurable, achievable, relevant, and time-bound). Having defined goals helps to prevent uncertainty and gives an objective.

Mission of segmentation

Divide more ambitious objectives into more manageable chores. Doing these tiny chores can increase motivation and lessen the psychological resistance to larger jobs.

Positive Self-Talk: Adapt your perspective to become more driven

Your self-talk has an impact on your motivation and behaviour. By reframing negative ideas, positive self-talk encourages a growth mentality that inspires tenacity and perseverance.

Displacing restrictive beliefs

Identify negative thoughts that get in the way of your motivation, such as "I could never do this." Present proof of prior accomplishments and advancements to refute these misconceptions.

Affirmations Make up encouraging statements to bolster your resolve and capacity to achieve your objectives. Repeat these statements frequently to help cultivate an attitude of confidence.

Reward Scheme: Progress-based

Setting up reward programmes for reaching goals gives people concrete incentives that support and encourage productive conduct.

Rewards that arrive right away or take time to arrive

Strike a balance between rewards that happen immediately, like quick breaks, and rewards that take time, like finishing a project or reaching a goal. While delayed rewards foster long-term engagement, immediate rewards offer quick gratification.

Honouring advancement

Keep yourself motivated, recognise your efforts, and celebrate even small victories. Realising your success gives you a greater sense of achievement and encourages you to keep going.

Accountability of Partners and Public Promise: Motivation from without

By involving outside motivators, such as accountability partners or public participation, you reduce procrastination and maintain accountability for your tasks.

Partner for accountability

Discuss your objectives and advancement with a confidant who will ensure your responsibility. Frequent check-ins instil accountability and inspire obedience.

Public endorsement

Make your objectives known to friends, family, and coworkers in public. Your accountability and determination are strengthened when you are dedicated to realising your goals in front of the public.

Focus on the tasks that will have the most impact by applying the 80/20 rule. It is a theory that states that, for every given event, 20% of all causes (or inputs) account for 80% of the outputs.

In the business world, this frequently means that 20% of consumers account for 80% of income or 20% of clients account for 80% of complaints. However, regarding individual productivity, it suggests that 20% of your efforts provide 80% of the benefits. This principle's simplicity and universality are what makes it so beautiful. This heuristic applies to almost every field, including business, economics, personal productivity, and lifestyle management. Finding and concentrating on the 20% of tasks that will result in 80% of your intended outcomes is crucial.

For example, think about an average weekday. Most people feel they have a long list of things they need to do. Nonetheless, the Pareto Principle states that the most significant outcomes will come from a tiny percentage of these tasks. You can significantly increase your efficiency and production by identifying and concentrating on these high-impact jobs.

It's important to have a solid grasp of your objectives and the essential steps in reaching them to pinpoint the 20% of your efforts that yield 80% of your outcomes. This is figuring out what success means to you:

Developing your business

Getting forward in your work

Getting healthier

Strengthening your bonds with others

After your objectives are clear, you can work backwards to determine the crucial actions that will enable you to reach your goals.

For instance, closing deals can be your ultimate objective if you work in sales. But not every sales-related duty is equally important. While responding to emails, going to meetings, and writing reports are all necessary tasks for the work, developing connections with important clients or providing product demos may be the actions that result in the closure of sales. These are probably the 20% of work you should concentrate on the most.

Using the 80/20 rule to prioritise your duties can also help you avoid burnout and minimise stress. You can free up time and lessen the sensation of being overwhelmed by concentrating on the things that matter and getting rid of or assigning less important responsibilities. Though, it does not imply that you should disregard the other 80% of the work. You can use it as a guide to prioritise and concentrate on high-impact projects. The precise ratio will probably change based on the circumstances. All the principle does is make you carefully consider where you spend your time and energy.

In conclusion, you can improve your productivity by concentrating on the things that impact your job and life by implementing the 80/20 rule. It's an effective tool that will help you work smarter, not harder, in time management, goal-setting, and decision-making.

Make the most of your commute by tuning into podcasts or audiobooks.

Many people consider the daily commute to be a monotonous and wasteful period that comes after the workday. It's a place of change, where obligations from the personal to the professional spheres are marked, and vice versa. On the other hand, the commute may become an enjoyable and productive portion of the day with a little imagination and perspective adjustment. Make use of podcasts and audiobooks as a means of accomplishing this shift.

Podcasts and audiobooks may transform your commute into an insightful class on nearly any topic, a personal development seminar, or a riveting novel experience. They make it possible to absorb knowledge, perspectives, and narratives in a period that would otherwise be wasted aimlessly. This can enhance your commute enjoyment and advance your career and personal development.

Audiobooks are an excellent method to enjoy literature when it is difficult to find the time to read books in print. They can help you discover new horizons, examine various viewpoints, and deepen your comprehension of various cultures, eras, or intellectual disciplines. Audiobooks may transform your commute into an educational experience, whether listening to a self-help book, a classic novel, a modern work of fiction, or non-fiction on a subject you're interested in learning more about.

Conversely, podcasts provide vast content suitable for nearly every interest. Science, technology, history, philosophy, psychology, business and entrepreneurship, and more. Podcasts that give insights and guidance for both personal and professional growth often include interviews with influential people, experts, and leaders in the field. Others share thought-provoking narratives, arguments, or investigations of difficult subjects; they can broaden your understanding and encourage critical thought.

While commuting, listening to podcasts or audiobooks can also be beneficial psychologically. It can make the commute more enjoyable by diverting your attention from the strain or boredom of the commute. Engaging with intellectually intriguing content can also assist in maintaining mental acuity and cultivating a curiosity and a never-ending learning mindset.

Obtaining audiobooks and podcasts in the digital era is easier than ever. A wide range of content is available on several platforms, frequently for free or at a low monthly membership cost. A mobile device and some headphones are all you need.

But it's crucial to remember that safety should always come first. Ensure your podcast or audiobook is ready to go before you start driving, and never allow it to take your attention away from the road. Ensure your possessions are secure, and pay attention to your surroundings when taking public transportation.

In conclusion, even though the commute might seem necessary, audiobooks and podcasts can make it a worthwhile and meaningful portion of your day. Travelling can become an opportunity for research and growth with various mediums, whether your goal is to study, develop, or just pass the time.

The Success Blueprint: Time Management Foundations For A Busy Life

While it's a necessary skill for everyone, entrepreneurs and students, in particular, need to know how to manage their time well. You can maximise the value of your time and complete tasks faster with time management. By concentrating on what matters, it can also aid in the development of self-discipline and enhance interpersonal connections.

Setting realistic goals.

You won't know what you want to accomplish if you don't set goals. It is useless to work towards your objective if you cannot monitor your advancement. Furthermore, setting an unrealistically high standard for yourself will only lead to self-doubt and anger when things don't work out as you had hoped. So, how can we determine what is reasonable? Well, the first thing to do is to figure out how long something will take. As an illustration, A one-minute activity should take sixty seconds; a ten-minute task should take no more than nine and fifty-nine seconds (or so).

Acquiring the ability to refuse.

Although no one likes saying no, we must all occasionally do so. Developing the habit of saying no is the best method to improve your ability to say no.

Here's where to begin:

● Begin modestly by declining little requests like dinner reservations or non-urgent favours. Everyone has to ask for help occasionally; friends and family members can easily exploit this reality. Refuse to give in to this kind of pressure; maintain your routine and graciously turn down requests that conflict with your regular activities. This will help you become more confident in your abilities to say no to bigger requests in the future!

Maintaining a to-do list.

The foundation of any time management strategy is the to-do list. It organises all the tasks you must complete so you can concentrate on finishing them. How will you remember where things are if you don't have a to-do list?

It's crucial to avoid adding too many chores to your lists. Many times, people attempting new time management and productivity techniques feel overburdened by everything they have to get done in a single day. Because they have too much on their plate at once, and we all know how frustrating that can be, this causes them to give up easily. Rather, concentrate on the most crucial task first thing in the morning: making a detailed schedule for your day with a specific goal in mind (such as "finish project"). Then, as new activities (like "call client") or completed tasks (like "upload presentation") arise throughout the day, make sure these are added to your master list as needed to ensure that nothing is overlooked. For example, you should call clients after lunch rather than earlier because there's no excuse not to!

Setting work priorities.

Setting priorities for your work is one of the most crucial time management techniques. You must first identify your priorities if you want to execute this effectively. Depending on the circumstances, your goals may vary from day to day or from hour to hour.

Using a priority matrix, which divides all your jobs into high- and low-priority categories, is a useful method for task prioritisation. In this matrix, every task has a single spot. Therefore, if a task has two priorities, sleep and high priorities, it gets two spaces! When making decisions about what needs to be done when it's not covered by other assignments ahead of time by default order, you should also assign multiple spots to items that have similar levels of importance, like eating lunch, so that they can be easily remembered later on without requiring you to look back through everything else written down.

Controlling interruptions and putting off tasks.

Distractions might undermine your efforts to complete tasks. Everybody is faced with several jobs at once. Sometimes, we must put down our work and focus on something else. But the diversion turns into procrastination—it stops being beneficial and begins to be detrimental—when we have only one task left on our plate, and it won't go away until we accomplish it.

You may be having trouble controlling distractions and procrastination if you switch between projects frequently or allow little things to pull you away from your main objective. You may also struggle if: ● You have problems starting or finishing projects because they're too vast or intimidating; ● You can't figure out how to prioritise your time; or even worse...

The development of time management skills can take years. Use these building blocks as a starting point to enhance your talents.

● Begin with one thing. ● Divide your work into manageable chunks. ● Track your development and acknowledge it!

The secret is to recognise how you spend your time and determine how to use it better.

The secret is to recognise how you spend your time and determine how to use it better. You'll probably find that some items on your list are not that vital when you start looking at this; they could be time-consuming chores that don't add anything to the rest of your day.

Which five elements make up goal-setting?

The fundamental goal requirements are S.M.A.R.T. objectives—specific, measurable, achievable, relevant, and time-bound. These five standards ensure the goals are relevant and centre around the team members and the business's overall professional development.

Particular

Any goal that requires development needs to have a clear destination. Whether the objective is to launch a new product, boost sales, or soothe customer worries, being as specific as possible about the target improves project planning and execution.

Quantifiable

It's not always feasible to quantify results or even precise objectives. Managers and leaders must start over and establish a new goal if this is the case. If results are far below expectations, managers and other leaders can intervene. Teams can utilise a progress monitoring technique to see whether they are headed in the right direction.

Realistic

When fair but slightly unachievable goals are maintained, workers stay focused and support the development of their talents.

Creating ten thousand audio cassettes daily is a specific, measurable, and achievable goal, but is it relevant? Set goals and monitor metrics to keep staff members engaged, but little progress will be achieved. Companies need to be on the lookout for fresh approaches to stay innovative.

Time-limited

Wishes are all that ambitious ambitions with no deadline are. Managers and team members will most likely put off accomplishing the goals if there is no deadline.

Purposeful goals are the foundation of effective ones. The ability of managers to create objectives and associated benchmarks aids teams tremendously in locating any bottlenecks, capitalising on momentum, and accomplishing the intended result. They aim to help managers make plans, not merely wish and fantasise.

Setting goals is crucial for any organisation.

As organisations become closer to adopting a hybrid working style, managers are more responsible for giving their team members the greatest support available. With extensive goal planning that considers crucial results and tracking technologies, this "monitored autonomy" can be effectively applied to workers' and managers' routine responsibilities. Managers can set realistic expectations and give their staff the freedom to succeed by creating S.M.A.R.T. goals. Well-known businesses like Microsoft and Google are putting into practice plans based on concepts covered in Dan Pink's Ted Talk regarding the significance of autonomy for motivation. These companies aim to give employees greater control over their tasks, responsibilities, and goals.

In addition to offering clarity and motivation, employee goals help employees complete their work more successfully. Studies show that when creating staff goals, it is critical to ensure that all involved are dedicated to reaching them and actively desire to do so. Managers and leaders can help by getting a sense of what is meaningful, satisfying, or compatible with the personal beliefs of their staff members.

According to a Deloitte survey, an increasing proportion of millennial employees recognise their value in the workplace and are committed to upholding the company's mission and values.

Turn to page eight.

Time management for solopreneurs: To free up time for strategic endeavours and business expansion, automate repetitive duties via workflows and systems.

Time Management and Personal Efficiency Metrics: To monitor your development, track personal efficiency metrics like the amount of work finished in an hour or the proportion of time dedicated to high-priority tasks.

Investor Time Management: To ensure they make well-informed investment decisions, investors should set aside specific time for financial analysis, portfolio management, and research.

Time management and time zones: To facilitate collaboration when working with individuals in various time zones, employ scheduling tools and apps that consider these variances.

Time management and Mental Health Breaks: Schedule regular times for mental health breaks. Taking brief pauses for deep breathing, mindfulness, or meditation can improve well-being and productivity.

Finding your natural circadian cycles and peak performance periods is important for time management. Plan your most difficult assignments for these periods to maximise your physical and mental resources.

Time Management and Time-Blocking Themes: Schedule time for days or weeks using a theme. For instance, you may set off a day or a week to plan strategically or generate innovative ideas.

Time Management for Consultants: By focusing on a particular area of expertise and keeping up to date with new developments, consultants can make the most of their time. They can work more productively and provide clients with greater value.

Time Management and Passion Projects: Set aside time for your passion projects, such as writing a book, launching a side business, or engaging in creative work.

Time Management to Advance Your Career: To further your professional development, set aside regular time for activities like skill development, networking, and career planning.

Time management and Agile Life Planning: Apply the concepts of agile life planning derived from agile project management. Accept flexibility and the need for ongoing development in your personal and professional life.

Time Management for Public Speakers: It is advantageous for presenters to plan and practise their speeches well in advance. Allocate dedicated time for producing material, honing delivery techniques, and practising.

Time Management and Overseeing Multiple Businesses: If you oversee several businesses or endeavours, assign lower-priority work to others and concentrate on the activities that will influence each organisation the most.

Time Management for Researchers: To make their jobs go more smoothly, researchers can employ organised research approaches, project management software, and reference management systems.

Time management and the "Do Not Disturb" technique: Set aside time during your busiest work hours for "Do Not Disturb" periods. To reduce disruptions, let coworkers or family members know about this.

Time Management for Nonprofits: To manage fundraising initiatives and community involvement effectively, nonprofit managers can use volunteer coordination tools and donor management software.

Time management and self-care retreats: To refuel and revitalise, plan recurring self-care retreats. These retreats might help you maintain balance and perspective.

Time Management for Family Life: To efficiently manage family obligations and responsibilities, implement time management principles in your home by creating routines, shared calendars, and communication channels.

Time management and crisis response: When faced with a crisis, deploy crisis response strategies and protocols to quickly assign resources and deal with pressing problems.

Time management and legacy planning: Consider your long-term impact and set aside time for legacy-building pursuits like community service, philanthropy, and mentorship.